Attention

The Atom of Consciousness

Ido Angel

Ido Angel
Attention:
The Atom of Consciousness

Published by Spines
ISBN: 979-8-89383-770-4

Attention

The Atom of Consciousness

Ido Angel

Contents

Part One
Outward

Part Two
Inward

Introduction

Draw Me a Table

When we talk about attention, we usually refer to an action related to our conscious ability to focus our spotlight of discernment, to concentrate on something in such a way that allows us a clearer view of its properties, properties that are not immediately apparent and would not emerge in a casual glance. We associate our attention with intention: I intend to be a better husband to my wife, so I will try to pay attention to her words; I certainly do not intend to buy an electric nose hair trimmer in the near future, so I will not pay attention to the myriad ads that pop up before my eyes on social networks. Attention is something we perceive in our minds as something we can control, or at least regulate. This is "discriminative" attention because its action is to discern something that is already present; we just need to pay attention to it so that we can discern it. This attention requires consciousness in order to exist; whether it occurs consciously or subconsciously, its result generates an experience—an experience of discernment—and an experience exists only in a self-aware consciousness.

In this essay, I propose a completely different type of attention. This is attention that occurs on a completely different plane of reality from that discriminative attention we tend to call "mindfulness". This statement does not contain anything spiritual or mystical. I am talking about a simple and self-evident fact; all one needs to do is look at reality with clear eyes—put aside our experience of reality and look at reality as it truly is. This attention can be called "universal-creative attention."

In our experience, what constitutes reality? The immediate answer would be: things. We adopt a Bottom Up approach and depict the universe as constructed in such a way that the smallest things make up the slightly larger things, and these make up the slightly larger things, and so on until the largest thing, which is the universe itself. If we take the human body as an example, we could say that subatomic particles make up molecules, which make up cells, which make up various materials such as bones, muscles, blood, brain, eyes, etc., which in turn make up the thing called "the body". The same applies to plants, soil, clouds, air, electricity, black holes. This is a very convenient approach because it is very useful: it gives us control over reality. The fundamental laws of the universe tell us how things behave with each other, and thus we can predict our future: we can plan a spacecraft landing on the moon and on Mars, we can deflect an asteroid from its collision course with Earth, we can defeat viruses, know what the weather will be tomorrow, and even ease our minds with good advice—all because reality is made up of things whose behavior we can predict based on their adherence to the fixed and known laws of physics. But here is an interesting question: if things constantly react to each other, if they are in perpetual interaction with one another—doesn't that mean that all things are in a state of constant change? Even the smallest particles react to each other—electromagnetic fields change, structural deformations occur, bosons move from one particle to another, energy weakens or intensifies. Nothing is free from change. So, can we really call anything a "thing"?

Take, for example, a table (after all, we always take a table as an example). The table is made, among other things, of wood. When did the wood become a table? Was it at the last sanding stroke of the carpenter who made it? Was it when it was first used? And when did the wood itself become wood? Was it when the seed was planted in the ground? Was it when it sprouted for the first time? There is no clear point like this—not in the past, and not in the future. Surely, in 10 million years, the table will no longer be a table. It will probably become dust that will scatter across the universe. When does this process of the table becoming dust begin? The answer is that it never begins. It is a continuous process that began with the birth of the universe and its end is unknown. Every table is already dust in the making. It is very convenient for us to draw a table with chalk on the board and say, "This is a drawing of a table." But isn't the "real" table, the one we place our objects on, also just a drawing? Is the word "table" merely a decision we made in our minds, a utilitarian decision that ignores the simple truth that, in the raw essence of reality as it is, there is no "table"?

These are not new questions. The philosopher Gottfried Wilhelm Leibniz said similar things regarding matter, but he was not the first; Siddhartha Gautama, known as the "Buddha," said this more than 2500 years ago: things have no separate self-identity, and nothing is permanent. Everything is in constant flux, and all things are interconnected. Modern science also supports this view. Theoretical physicist Carlo Rovelli states: "reality is not made of things but of interactions." Remember the child in the movie "The Matrix"? "There is no spoon," he tells Neo, meaning exactly that: the spoon is merely a utilitarian—but baseless—freeze-frame of reality.

But wait. If reality is not made of things but of interactions—between what does the interaction take place? What reacts to what if not... things? We are caught in a paradox. On the one hand, the very fact that things interact with each other blurs to the point of nullifying their existence as things, i.e., objects with separate and fixed self-identity; but on the other hand, if things are not things at all, interactions cannot occur, the "action" must happen "inter", between one thing and another. So what is really happening here? After all, there is someone writing these words—it is me—I have a fairly certain and real sense of existence. Also, this table—if I ignore its status as a thing and try to walk through it, it will hurt. So if there is no "me," if there is no table, if there is no interaction between me and the table—why would it hurt so much? What on earth exists?

The answer this essay proposes to this question is a different kind of attention—universal-creative attention. To understand this answer, we must fundamentally understand what this attention truly is—what its role is, how and on whom it acts, and what the significance of this insight is for the universe in general and for us in particular. This is an attention different from discriminative attention. It is an attention whose concern is not to discern something already present but to create its presence (hence "creative"). It is an attention that does not need experience to occur, and thus it can occur in everything (hence "universal"). Again, this is not a spiritual or religious insight, but on the other hand, I am not sure any immediate scientific profit can be derived from it. It is a different observation of how our reality works, an observation whose essence is not necessarily an answer but a question.

An important note before we begin: in many places, I have chosen to use the Hebrew term "Tsumat Lev" for the word attention because, as will be explained in detail later, it serves as a very efficient linguistic lever for the conceptual thrust I am trying to demonstrate.

I would like to thank everyone who helped bring this essay to light: Professor Avi Elkayam and the Idra Publishing House with all its staff. To Roni Somek and Nir Stern, who greatly contributed to the second part of the book, and to Merav Schreiber, who generously shared with me interesting insights on attention in the most human sense of the term. I thank Roni Avni for proofreading the Hebrew version of this essay. I thank my friend Oren Lavie for weaving his heart with mine. I thank my family—my beloved children and my wife, without whom I would be a distant observer in this world.

Part One

Outward

The Sense of Being Stared At

The first time the term "attention", well, caught my attention, was during a random YouTube lecture given by Dr. Rupert Sheldrake. The phenomenon he attempted to investigate was nothing less than telepathy.

I consider myself a relatively open-minded person. My lifelong engagement with literature and poetry might indicate an active right brain; I enjoy delving into questions related to consciousness, free will, belief, and I always tend to seek the connection between the rational and the abstract. However, when a concept like "telepathy" suddenly comes up, I start to shift uncomfortably in my chair.

But I fell in love with Sheldrake quite easily. He is an empirical biologist, rigorously methodical, who for many years carried the feeling that all this science, which was his daily bread, easily dismissed questions related to experiences that pulse in every person's life, certainly in his own. The ways in which science views many subjects seemed increasingly rigid to Sheldrake, to the point that when they led to dead ends or internal contradictions, science, or at least scientists, preferred "not to be confused by the facts," as the saying goes, and stuck to the safer, clearer places without questioning their truths even for a moment.

This bothered him for a while until one day he decided to take action. He would address these contradictions himself and perhaps even find a way to reconcile them. He started with questions from home, questions related to his main field of study, biology. For example, he asked, "Why is genealogy not sufficient to explain plant evolution?" But soon, he expanded to more distant (and some would say even dubious) realms, such as the question "How can it be that people feel when someone is looking at them?" or "How can it be that you think of someone just before they call you?" As an empiricist, he began conducting experiments.

To test the phone issue, for example, he organized an experiment like this: he asked a person (let's call him George for demonstration purposes) to choose four people close to him, genetically or socially, meaning people with whom he had some degree of relationship or affection. Then George was placed in a sealed room with an old rotary phone, incapable of identifying incoming calls. The four people George chose were initially selected from various distant locations, some even on different continents. To dispel any suspicion of human bias, each of them was randomly instructed to call George in turn. When George picked up the receiver, he had to first say the name of the caller who came to his mind, based solely on his feeling.

Any reasonable person would say that George's chance of correctly identifying the caller's name is 1 in 4, or 25%. But Sheldrake's experiment showed otherwise. George, and not only him but all the other "Georges" chosen for the experiment, hit the correct name 45% of the time. This is an astonishing figure by any measure. But that's not what is truly amazing. What was remarkable about Sheldrake's experiment was that when four completely unknown people to George were chosen for the experiment, meaning people George did not know at all, the hit rates aligned with the expected 25% probability. Sheldrake demonstrated a significant correlation between George's closeness to the people he chose and his ability to sense who among them called him.

Sheldrake explains the results of the experiment (and many others he conducted) with an intriguing term he coined: "Morphic Resonance." Briefly and grossly simplifying the subject—Sheldrake argues that our brain is not only within our body but can also resonate outside it, especially with those who are "morphically" close to us, meaning those who share some patterns with us, expressed in our connection, affection, similar habits, or some genetic schema. According to Sheldrake, morphic resonance operates based on memory stored in a field, so that the echoes are actually memory echoes of the experiences we had together, behaving as a kind of carriers of our brain activity outside our body.

This is an ambiguous and fascinating theory, and many would undoubtedly consider it pseudoscientific. But none of this matters. What resonated in my mind after the lecture ended was a seemingly minor term Sheldrake mentioned during his talk. Sheldrake said something like, "Morphic resonance occurs when both parties are in attention to each other"—and I felt as if something struck me, not necessarily because of the "Sheldrakean" context of the sentence I had just heard. The term "attention" seemed to float slightly before the computer screen, stared at me for a moment, and then smiled, as if to say: "Hey, Ido. Yes, you're thinking in the right direction."

The Hard Problem

The "hard problem" of science, a term coined by philosopher David Chalmers in 1995, is related to the very subjective experience itself, which cannot be explained using conventional objective scientific tools. The fact that the experience itself exists for a particular organism, even if the objective explanation for this existence is purely mechanical-functional, means that there is something it is like to be that organism. But how can we objectively-functionally explain an experience that is entirely subjective, whose subjectivity is its very essence? Chalmers argues that the only way to do this is to include the experience itself as a fundamental component of existence, on par with space, mass, and time, and not dismiss it as an emergent phenomenon arising from physical activity, like wetness, which is not found in a single water molecule but emerges from the combination of water molecules.

Chalmers offers an interesting way to bridge the gap between subjective experience and objective physical processes: information. Information has two aspects—on one side, it carries the description of the external aspect of things, i.e., physics, while the other side is responsible for describing their internal aspect, i.e., experience.

Giulio Tononi, a psychiatrist and neuroscientist, also makes a similar argument and has even founded a theory called the "Integrated Information Theory," whose sole purpose is to provide solutions to Chalmers' hard problem and explain not how the brain works when consciousness occurs, but how consciousness itself operates, and even measure different levels of consciousness in various entities—human, worm, or even a computer program—using the symbol Φ (phi).

These are topics on which many books have been written, and we are passing over them quickly, undoubtedly doing a great injustice to the people who conceived them. But that's okay. This is not the main focus of this essay. Right now, the important point for us is this: information is present in everything.

In computer language, the meaning of the word "information" is related to data processing. "Processing" is receiving a given piece of data, translating it, and then passing the translation along. The word "information" describes the process precisely: in(to)-form—this is an action that involves translating a certain piece of data (content) into another language (form).

When we say that information is present in everything, what exactly do we mean? We mean that everything carries information. For example, every stone has mass. A glass shattering on the floor, due to the myriad interactions occurring during the shattering event, carries information about its falling speed, the relationship between that speed and the glass's thickness, the material from which the floor is made, the height from which it fell. But is consciousness also present in everything that carries information?

When data processing is complex, like in the human brain, there is certainly consciousness, for there is experience. But what happens when the experience is simpler, like in a worm? And what about when there is no experience at all, like in a flower? A stone? An atom? And what about really large things that contain conscious entities within them, like a group of people? A group of planets? A galaxy? Space itself? Time?

Tononi argues that "conscious" processing of information occurs only when the system knows how to translate the symbols into meaning—into experience. In this sense, a computer program does not carry consciousness because its only action is to translate symbols into other symbols. But when a bat translates the information of the sonar wave returning from the object it projected into an experience, it is conscious. In this essay, I wish to ask a follow-up question or propose an additional perspective related to the system of processing data into information: I want to argue that perhaps "awareness" is not present in everything, but there is a fundamental level of data processing that is not "symbol to symbol," and it necessarily exists in every single thing in the cosmos, whether the thing is capable of being aware of this process or not, meaning whether it experiences it subjectively or not—whether it is the smallest particle, inanimate objects, organic systems like plants, animals, humans, and of course the entire universe itself.

The meaning of the Latin word "datum" is "a given thing", something that is as it is, that has not undergone any manipulation, something raw that has not yet been processed. Data is an abstract thing, while information is concrete. An equation, for example, is data. x=y. Neither of the equation's members has a known and defined value. But if this data were joined by another piece of data, for example, that the value of x is 2, then the two data points could be processed to calculate the equal value of y in this case.

At the beginning of the essay, we asked: if reality is not made up of things but of interactions—between what does the interaction take place? Well, the interaction is an event of data processing. At one end, an input of abstract data without value enters, and at the other end, an output of concrete, measured information emerges.

When two magnets are placed close to each other, if their poles have the same magnetic sign, they will repel each other, and if the poles have different magnetic signs, they will attract each other. In both interactions, data processing takes place. The data is the equations according to which different polarities act on each other in a certain way, while the actual result of attraction or repulsion with specific intensity is the information. During the interaction, each magnet "holds" information about the other. And I want to argue that the fist holding this information is attention.

The Atom of Consciousness

Experiments in epigenetics (a field in biology that deals with changes in gene function that are not associated with changes in the DNA sequence but rather with the suppression or enhancement of certain genes) conducted on mice with identical genetic load showed that following a traumatic experience, only some of the mice developed symptoms of anxiety. The mice that survived the trauma with almost no symptoms at all were those whose mothers licked them. However, this is not where the experiment ends: the anxiety symptoms developed by the mice whose mothers did not lick them were inherited by their offspring and even their grandchildren.

Apparently, we see here a demonstration of the power of attention in its common, controlled, discriminative sense —the conscious ability to focus our spotlight of distinction on something. The mother mouse directed her full attention to her offspring's needs and provided him with the security he needed at a moment of crisis. However, in a moment, we shall see that the "other" kind of attention, the one this essay aims to show that occurs consciously or not in everything across the universe, is also demonstrated here, and even more powerfully.

But let's start with the "ordinary" attention. One can say that the attention the mother mouse gave her offspring, or in other words, the experience the mouse offspring had thanks to the attention his mother gave him, caused a change not only in his psyche but also in his body, just as the traumatic experience caused a change in the bodies of the other mice, those who were not given the same attention, to the point where the anxiety symptoms they developed were passed on to future generations. In other words, one can say that the experiment proves that the experiential aspect affects the material aspect.

Such a perception challenges the Darwinian view prevailing in most scientific circles. Darwin argued that all genetic changes occur randomly and that eventually, the mutations that underwent a genetic change that contributed to their survival (again, randomly) are simply those that indeed survived, while the rest perished (also randomly) from the world. For illustration, different giraffes were born randomly with necks of different lengths, but only the giraffes with the longer necks survived because they were the ones who could reach the leaves on the high trees and eat them. The giraffes that were randomly born with shorter necks became extinct, and this is Darwinian evolution in its simplicity. In contrast, in the early 19th century, the researcher Jean-Baptiste Lamarck argued that giraffes with short necks developed longer necks over the years not randomly at all, but because when they tried to reach the leaves on the high trees, they stretched their necks, and the stretching itself, which became a habit, created a physiological change that was imprinted and preserved for future generations; each generation was born with a neck longer than the previous one until the long necks became fixed to the right extent. In other words, the need to survive gave birth to the necessary biological tools.

Science, as mentioned, sided with Darwin. But epigenetics brings us back to the point where the question is asked: to what extent do our experiences, internal and external, affect our bodies—and not just affect them, but actually change them. Although they do not change the genetic sequence, the building materials themselves, but the genetic emphasis, the way these materials are used; certain genes "turn on" and others "turn off". But the change is significant enough to roll down the genetic path and even influence future generations.

But—the reductionist will say—after all, the experience itself is also material, or at least it occurs in material. The right areas in the brain "light up" and then command other areas responsible for different functions. Symbol responds to symbol. The fact that the giraffe "wanted" to eat, that is, experienced hunger, does not matter at all.

Even if the need to eat was not experienced by the giraffe as the experience of "I feel hungry", the body would still signal the brain that it needs to get food, more or less as a car signals that it is out of fuel, and the brain would respond to the need in a completely technical manner without any subjective experience echoing in it and would send the body to gather food.

This is a lively and interesting philosophical question in the field of consciousness research. It is called the "philosophical zombie question". Imagine a creature identical to a human being but devoid of any subjective experience. A zombie. The behavior of the zombie is identical to that of the conscious human, but unlike him, the zombie experiences nothing "inside". Do we have a way to know that all the people who are not us are not actually some kind of philosophical zombies? This question preoccupies many philosophers, including Chalmers. We will not pretend to answer it here—but we will ask: so what? This is seemingly an arrogant or indifferent question, but it is important because any answer we give to the question of the influence of experience on matter, and in general, any answer we give regarding the nature of consciousness, will match the "other" universal attention and its mode of operation in reality. Even the staunchest reductionist will not be able to interfere with the process this essay seeks to present because reductionism does not refute or contradict it; on the contrary, the "universal" attention seeks to stand firm and existent even in the face of such a perception and also in the eyes of anyone who believes that subjective experience itself is a fundamental component of the universe.

To explain this, let's return to our mouse, but this time we will not talk about the love his mother showered on him and the experience he had. We will talk about something much much smaller: a neuron.

One can explain the operation of a neuron in several ways. Let's imagine for a moment that we are a team of biologists and neuroscientists explaining the activity of a neuron in the mouse's brain, the same neuron that fired in response to the mother's touch and initiated a chain of actions that ultimately made the mouse's body more protected than the bodies of those mice whose neurons did not fire similarly because their mothers did not lick them. If we take a reductive-Darwinian approach, we would say that the neuron fired simply because it is coded to do so, and it is coded this way by virtue of an evolutionary survival mechanism that developed entirely by chance in nature. This is an external physical aspect. But this view only answers the question, "Why did the neuron react the way it did?" and does not answer the more interesting question: "What triggered the neuron's response to the mother's touch?" What is the processing mechanism within the neuron where touch enters on one side, and a firing occurs on the other? Well, the neuron pays attention. This may sound too simple and obvious—the touch occurred, the neuron noticed it (because it is coded that way), and therefore it fired. But when we say this, we do not mean that the neuron really noticed something in the same way the mother mouse noticed her son. This is just a figure of speech. The neuron has no consciousness, so it cannot perform a conscious action like discriminative attention; it has no mindfulness that it can focus, no intention. So what really happened there? How did the neuron pay attention after all?

Let's be strict with ourselves for a moment. Let's say that the neuron simply "reacted" without any awareness or consciousness, just like our philosophical zombie or like a stone that shatters when struck with a hammer, not knowing it is shattering, without a shred of experience, simply obeying the cold laws of physics. But wait. Earlier we said that laws tell us about the nature of interactions, and an interaction is a data processing system that produces information. Like the glass we mentioned in the previous chapter, the stone has a certain mass; so does the hammer moving towards the stone at a certain speed, and both are located at specific coordinates in space. The "conversation" between all these pieces of data–i.e., the specific compliance of this specific stone and this specific hammer to the laws of physics–is not to be taken for granted because it happens only during their specific interaction. This is a one-time conversation. Of course, outside this interaction, the stone and the hammer continuously and ceaselessly obey other laws related to other interactions. The stone obeys gravity; the hammer's wood obeys entropy, it reacts to heat, air, moisture. In other words, interactions are what "realize" the laws of physics; they are what gives these pieces of data meaning in the physical world. In fact, data can only manifest in interaction—and interactions happen all the time—"there is no place devoid of it," as written in the Kabbalic Zohar book regarding the presence of God. The world is an endless sequence of one-time continuous conversations, and data has no value, it is impossible to say anything clear about it except in relation to other pieces of data, i.e., in the act of processing. "The stone's mass is x" only because there are other things with different masses. The stone is not "heavy" or "light" by itself. It is heavy only in relation to something lighter and light only in relation to something heavier. Its x does not stand alone as an independent, objective value. In fact, without interaction there is no stone at all. The stone is a process, and the process is a continuous sequence of interactions. In other words, even the cold, ceaseless obedience of all things to the laws of physics is not devoid of data processing into information, even at the lowest level, and this processing action creates meaning by giving value to the data themselves. This is attention. There is nothing mental or conscious here. This is a physical correlation between systems. But here's something interesting: the response does not necessarily contain any subjective experience, nevertheless, when we talk about such interaction, we have no linguistic way to describe it except as a conscious experience.

When ultraviolet light is projected onto metal, the metal reacts to it, as does the air around the metal. In the external aspect, it is possible to explain completely mechanically how the air and the metal behave when they react to the ultraviolet light. But in the internal aspect, we have no other way but to say that the air and the metal pay attention to the light. We can describe mechanically how things work—how the neuron fires, how a cell reacts to light in photosynthesis. We can even say "for what purpose" it acts this way. These are the "easy problems." But we have no other way to talk about what triggers the response of anything to anything else without referring to the thing linguistically as possessing some form of consciousness. Not awareness—but consciousness. We have no way to say anything about it without mentioning attention.

I remember listening to a lecture by Sam Harris, a neuroscientist, philosopher, and popular podcaster, in which he talked about free will, or more precisely, its absence. Harris is a proud atheist and reductionist. In the lecture, he tried to explain the fact that our thoughts are not "thought" by us, meaning there is no "super thinker" outside us who thinks our thoughts and bestows them into our brains. Just as the neuron simply reacts, so do thoughts simply appear. There is a lot of truth in this because even if there should be such an external thinker, unless it had its own external thinker, thoughts would ultimately have to simply emerge within him. But when Harris explained this, he phrased it in a very specific way, simply because he could not have phrased it otherwise. He said something like: "If we pay close attention to our thoughts, we will see that they just appear in our minds." Well, maybe there is no external thinker for thoughts, but there is attention to be paid in order to realize that. There has to be. And not only can we not consider the presence or absence of that external thinker without it, but we cannot talk about ourselves, lacking the external entity, without literally saying the opposite because "paying close attention to our thoughts" is a completely subjective action of observing ourselves from the outside. And if there is no external and internal—then who is paying attention to whom? And even if it is just a metaphor or a figure of speech to convey a certain idea (and that's what it probably is)—we still have no other way to talk about it or think about it differently. So maybe it is, simply, true? Maybe even a non-reflexive, truly "zombie" response can still be a response that contains a minimal but existing degree of consciousness, even if unaware? In other words—maybe there is no such thing as an absolute "zombie response" at all?

The perception that some degree of consciousness exists in everything is also not new, although it has gained momentum in recent years. It is called panpsychism, and it helps to answer a scientific conundrum that is a slightly different formulation of Chalmers' hard problem: how does the experience of consciousness emerge from a collection of unconscious particles? How many such particles would you need to "assemble" before consciousness would suddenly emerge from them? Well, if there is indeed some basic consciousness in every particle, then the path to more complex consciousness is paved much more easily.

This basic consciousness is attention. In this sense, we can say that universal-creative attention is "the atom of consciousness" because it exists wherever data processing occurs—meaning everywhere—both in complex data processing systems and in the simplest form of data processing. It exists in the neuron in the mouse's brain, it exists in the complete conscious unit of the mother mouse who pays attention to her son, it exists in biology, in physics, it is even present in cosmology—you could argue that gravity is spacetime's attention to matter or mass. It exists in the collapse of the wave function in quantum mechanics, which occurs only when the particle is measured—that is, when attention is paid to it. Attention, in short, is everywhere.

The Input of The Heart

In Hebrew, the term for "attention" is "Tsumat Lev." The word "Lev" means "heart." The word "Tsuma" is derived from the root "S-I-M", which means to place, or to put, but the actual term means "the total investment of resources required to produce output." Interestingly, this is the precise definition of the word "input." So our data processing system is naturally embodied in the Hebraic attention; "I was paying attention to the fact that you are behind me," "I am paying attention to the fact that I tend to speak loudly when I am happy," "I paid attention to the fact that your hair color has changed" – something was "placed inside" the heart, there was an in-put, something was absorbed and then integrated, a change that occurred in the fabric of reality – a change in the consciousness of the one who paid attention towards the presence of the thing they paid attention to, whether it is another entity ("I paid attention to the fact that Jack didn't come today") or a state ("I paid attention to the fact that every time the moon is full, I feel sad"). Data was processed into information.

Alongside the Hebrew expression, the roots of the English word "attention" reveal another aspect. The first root is the Latin word "ad," describing a movement towards something, and the second root is the word "ten," meaning "to stretch" (as in the word "tension"). In one common interpretation, the word "attention" can be presented as stretching towards something. But it can also be interpreted differently if we consider the original order of the roots, and thus instead of "stretching towards" (ten ad), the word means "towards the stretch" (ad ten), thereby emphasizing the intention to stretch, focusing on the slack before the stretch rather than the stretch itself.

When a string is slack, it does not produce a sound. The sound can only be heard when the string is taut. But "attention," in the etymologically ordered sense of its roots, does not describe a taut string, thus differing from the state of "paying attention", a phrase that carries some of the economic nuance of the Hebrew "Tsumat" for output. It is actually about the intention of the slack string to stretch towards something. Pay attention (!) that this is not absolute slackness but one where the stretch already "vibrates" within it precisely because of that intention.

In this essay, when we talk about attention, we will talk about "universal-creative attention" and refer to it as the mechanism responsible for the data processing into information present in every interaction. We will use the same "string" to describe the four stages of the process: its slackness, the intention charged in it to stretch between the sides at both ends, the actual stretch, and finally the tension. Only when the string is taut are we "fully attentive." We are already past the process that began with input; we are also past the paying – we have paid, and now we are ready for the output, the reward for our payment, a reward that in simple consciousness systems like particles comes in the form of cold compliance with the laws of nature, while in more complex consciousness systems like mice or humans, it is realized in the form of actual distinctive attention.

All this pertains to the first part of the Hebrew coupling "Tsumat Lev." But what about the second part? What is this thing we call "heart"?

The Heart

Let's further explore the string metaphor we presented. One end is held by the attention giver, i.e., the one who pays attention, and the other end is held by the receiver. Between them is the string. When the string is slack, nothing happens. The interaction between the holders at both ends does not occur, the data is not processed, and therefore no information is produced. Only when the string is taut does the interaction occur fully, the data is processed, information is created, value is given, and with it, meaning is generated. If sound cannot be played on a slack string, so too the information produced by the action of attention can only "vibrate" on a taut "attention string" and pass from one side to the other.

The slack string can serve as a metaphor for the quantum state called superposition, where a particle can be in several places simultaneously until it is measured.

In this metaphor, the taut string would be the single position of the particle after measurement, or "quantum" – after the wave function collapses. In the context of attention, slackness, like superposition, is the pre-concrete place where no distinction or differentiation exists, where things do not yet have names because in such a place things (as Rovelli argues) are not things at all. This is the heart.

When we talk about the heart, we are talking about what symbolizes the opposite of the mind, that is, the abstract which is the opposite of anything that has a name, definition, or logic. The "Heart Sutra" (or in its full name: "The Heart Sutra of Perfect Wisdom") is one of the most important and sacred sutras in Buddhism. It is written:

> *Do you know, Shariputra, what characterizes the emptiness of all truths? They neither arise nor cease, are neither defiled nor pure, and there is neither increase nor decrease in them. Therefore, in emptiness, there is no body, no feelings, desires, perceptions, or consciousness. No eye, ear, body, or mind, no form, sound, smell, taste, touch, or thought, and nothing is seen until the attainment of all-encompassing awareness. There is no ignorance and no end to ignorance, no aging and death and no end to aging and death.*

The sutra speaks of the heart as an empty place where no definition exists – but precisely because of this, it is an all-embracing place that holds within it wisdom greater than any definition or boundary that the mind can impose on things.

The Hebrew poet Chaim Nachman Bialik, in his wonderful essay "Revelation and Concealment in Language," writes:

> *It is clear that language, with all its combinations, does not bring us into the inner essence of things, but on the contrary, it itself forms a barrier before them. Outside the barrier of language, behind its veil, the human spirit, stripped of its verbal shell, is always wondering and wandering. There is no speech and there are no words, only eternal wonder; an eternal "what" frozen on the lips. In truth, there is no place even for that "what" which implies some hope for an answer.* [...] *If a person nonetheless comes to speak* [...] *it is only out of great fear of remaining for a moment with that dark "chaos"* [...] *face to face without a barrier. "For man shall not see me and live" – says the chaos, and every speech, every murmur of speech, is a cover,* [...] *a shell enclosing a dark drop of eternal lackness. No word completely nullifies any question, but what does it do? – it covers it.*

Bialik speaks of our fear of dwelling in that undefined chaos of the heart and how, out of fear, we use language whose whole purpose is to hide the chaos, to cover it. Words – that is, the mind – do not clarify anything for us. True, language is an efficient tool for conveying information, but does it alone generate meaning – or is it also just a translation "from symbol to symbol" while the meaning is created elsewhere? And perhaps language does create meaning – but as Bialik says, its action is precisely to use this meaning to cover something, not reveal it?

In Hebrew, "language" ("safa") is a synonym for "boundary". Language is a partition that separates the efficient yet cunning translation machine called "the mind" within the undefined chaos. You can see it in the most famous story of chaos, the story of the creation of the world.

In the first glance, the act of creation is the story of the six days when matter was created. But one can see it as the story of the creation of the mind or consciousness. In such a reading, "let there be light" does not mean the creation of light ex nihilo. It is an act of naming, a conscious act of delimiting, of creating a boundary in the unitary chaos, whose essence is distinguishing the phenomenon named "light" from all other phenomena that are not light. Just like the table mentioned in the introduction to the essay. Language separates, differentiates, discerns. "And God said" – God spoke, He used language to discern light from the chaos, and then continued to other things: "and God divided the waters which were under the firmament from the waters which were above the firmament" and so on and on to the separation of days from each other, the separation of the Tree of Knowledge from other trees, and finally the separation of man from other creatures and within that separation the separation of man from woman. The role of language, and hence of consciousness, is to distinguish – a useful and necessary role by all accounts, but it is important to understand that it also embodies concealment.

If we quickly return to Buddhism – according to the Buddha, the main cause of human suffering lies in an unclear, murky view of reality. We tend to see things as fixed and separate, while the truth is the exact opposite. We tend to believe in the separation made by the mind instead of understanding that its role, as necessary as it is, is not the whole truth. Separation gives us control but alongside it generates much suffering because when something is "a separate thing" we can cling to it and suffer when we fight endlessly against inevitable change.

Returning to Judaism. The word "heart" ("לב") itself is a word with special meaning. The first letter in the Hebrew Torah is "B" (in the word "Bereshit") and the last letter is "L" (in the word "Israel"), and together they form "B-L" or "L-B", לב, which is actually the entirety of the Torah, beginning to end. The "Book of Creation," attributed to Abraham, which mainly explains the creation of the world, begins with the words:

> *With thirty-two wondrous paths of wisdom engraved Yah, the Lord of Hosts, the God of Israel, the living God and King of the world, Almighty God, merciful and gracious, high and uplifted, dwelling in eternity, whose*

name is holy, He is lofty and holy, and He created His world...

Thirty-two, in numerology, is "לב" , and refer to the ten Kabbalistic sephirot and the twenty-two letters of the Hebrew alphabet. The heart is not only the content of creation but also the tool by which creation was brought into action – the letters that make up the language of words and numbers. The heart is the beginning, the way – but also the goal. And perhaps it is no coincidence that the Torah begins with the last letter of the word and ends with the first. Later we will see that attention is a two-way process – not only between the attention giver and the receiver but also in that to give its action real validity, the concrete produced by it must be somehow returned to the abstract. We will return to this.

So, the chaos, that is, the heart, is the data, the abstract data, and attention is the system that processes that data and produces information. What our eye absorbs when it encounters light rays reflected from objects is unprocessed data. This is the chaos. If this data were to meet a dead eye, for example, it would remain unprocessed and meaningless. But the living brain takes this data and processes it by doing exactly what was done in the act of creation – it categorizes and names it, thereby creating partitions to distinguish one piece from another and give them value and meaning, and then we can experience "table," "wall," "chair," etc.

This distinction occurs on three levels:

1. Distinguishing the thing to which attention is directed from other things (to which attention is not directed).
2. Distinguishing the giver (i.e., the one who pays attention) from the receiver (i.e., the one who is paid attention to).
3. Distinguishing each side (both the giver and the receiver) from their previous self, that is, from their self before attention was given.

To illustrate this clearly, let's return to our mouse: when the mother mouse paid attention to her son, the son mouse was distinguished from other mice whose mothers did not pay attention to. Similarly, in the act of attention, the son was distinguished from his mother – a necessary distinction whose purpose is not distance but rather closeness: if they were not separate from each other, the information (in this case, her love) could not pass from her to him, she could not give him anything. Third, the mouse that received attention is distinguished from itself before receiving attention, and the evidence for this is its effect on his soul and body, an effect that he will pass on to his descendants.

Heart Bit

Parmenides, the Greek philosopher, wrote: "What is, is, and what is not, is not." From this starting point he concluded that what is could never have come into being and must have existed forever, because if it had come into being, it must have come either from what is or from what is not - but what is not does not exist, so nothing can come from it. And if what is came from what is, then the question rolls back to earlier and earlier existences - what created the existence that created the existence?

The slackness of chaos, that "superpositional" slackness of our attention string, is not absolute nothingness. Indeed, it lacks specific value; it is not a thing, but it is also not nothing. It is a sort of formless potential, or more accurately, potentiality (since potential is a thing). It is the formless rawness of information.

The slackness of chaos is not subjective. No experience takes place within it. It holds no concrete information because it is itself the root of all information. Like superposition, it holds all possibilities, and because it lacks relation, no interaction occurs within it, and therefore no meaning is generated.

What is, is, meaning it is present. Just as water possesses the quality of wetness, so does "isness" possess the quality called "presence." Existence is not presence; I can exist without being present in a specific place. Presence is a quality that is inherently relative. It can never be general, detached from relation. It must be very specific.

In school, the teacher would read out the names of the students at the beginning of the lesson. This ceremony was called (translated from Hebrew) "presence check" back in my day. My response, "present!" to the sound of my name indicated my presence in relation to the class. Presence, according to the dictionary, is "being in a place." But pay attention (!) that the presence of a thing is verified not just in relation to the place where it is located but specifically in relation to the place where its presence is being checked. I can be present or not present only where my presence has been checked. In other places where my presence is not checked - I am neither present nor not present simply because no one checked it. For example, the empty space next to the curb existed for ages before I parked my car there. But it was not a parking spot and certainly not my parking spot. It became my parking spot only after I searched for and found it, just as an arbitrary room in an empty house is not a "kitchen," "living room," or "bathroom" until it is designated to be one of those.

In his wonderful book "How Are You, Dolores?" the Israeli author Yoel Hoffmann wrote:

> *Everything I enumerate is cut to the utmost perfection to the space allotted to it and to the order of time.*

There is no more precise sentence to describe presence - and even more so to describe the very act of making something present, that is, its emergence from chaos. The enumeration Hoffmann talks about is the act of processing data into concrete, valuable information. This is the paying of attention. But Hoffmann adds an important variable to the equation: for everything that is enumerated, there exists a special space and a special time allotted to it. The first action of the attention system is to identify that space which is "cut to the utmost perfection" to the dimensions of the thing it is making present, in order to turn chaotic slackness into "slackness intending to stretch." That space is a sort of chaotic template in the image of existence, into which and only into which it is poured. This is exactly the relativity needed for the emergence of presence. For a room to become a kitchen, the intention to turn it into one must first be identified, and not just any intention but that exact one from that exact thinker to that exact kitchen. And here, as if by magic, there is no more fitting manifestation of this process than a heartbeat, or a heart "bit", if you like: Outward (the blood exits) - space empties within the infinite chaos, an intention is created in the form of an empty template unique to the existence seeking to be present, then inward (the blood enters) - space fills the template, and now a thing "is present".

Take these very words that you are reading right now. Even before they were written and in order for me to be able to write them at all, to realize some "existence" that these words are the content of - I needed to have (in my heart) "allotted space and time" for them. It can also be phrased this way: my attention needed to be directed at the blank page, but not just any generic blank page, but the blank page of these exact words. Otherwise, how would I know what I want to write? This is the intention vibrating in the string. Only thus can "what is not written" ("what is slack") become "what is about to be written" ("what is about to stretch") - meaning that the precise intention "cut to the utmost perfection" will stretch in it and actually between us, me and the blank page, to turn in the following moments into "what is already written" - that is, to turn abstract data into concrete and meaningful information.

Those of you who write are surely asking: what needs to be done in order to pay attention to the "blank page of these exact words"? Simply put, nothing needs to be done. The attention we are talking about is not awareness; it is not a conscious and controlled act of focusing our discernment powers. As mentioned in the introduction, all this happens only later when our string is already taut, and the information can "vibrate" on it. When we decide to direct our spotlight of discernment, we are already listening to the sound playing on the taut string. The difference between attention and that conscious focus is somewhat like comparing money to the product it buys. Attention is not attentiveness; it is not noticing, and it is not even pre-attention, a concept from cognitive psychology emphasizing the separation existing in our minds between reactions we are aware of and those we are not aware of at all. The eye's response to a color shade deviating from a row of identical colors, or to a thicker line in a row of thin lines, or to movement in a static plane - all these are pre-attentive responses we are not necessarily aware of. The attention we are talking about here is closer to what American philosopher Ned Block calls "phenomenal consciousness", which precedes what he calls "access consciousness". Phenomenal consciousness does not precede access consciousness in a linear chain but is categorically different from it because it is not the action of consciousness but its essence. All conscious actions are by-products of it or, in our terms, its output. Attention is the phenomenon, while discernment is the action. Attention is what generates the discernment. When we listen to music, are we really listening to the music itself, or are we listening to ourselves, that is, to the interaction between us and the music, to the effect the music has on us, while to the music we are "merely" paying attention? Attention generates the interaction, and listening is the result of that interaction, it is the other end of this relationship that begins with attention.

Another way to demonstrate the template into which "things are cut to the utmost perfection" is related to the ancient Chinese concept of Yin-Yang. The literal meaning of the concept is "the dark side and the light side of the mountain." We are all well acquainted with the symbol, which has already been appropriated by Western culture and become very popular. But let's dwell on a few important things.

Perhaps the most essential thing from the perspective of the philosophy the symbol represents is that there is nothing in the entire universe that cannot be described with its help. Every thing has its opposite. Every phenomenon can be described with this simple binary of zero and one, of being and non-being. Even quantum superposition, where a particle can be in several places at once, is subject to the rule of Yin-Yang, for the opposite of superposition is the position itself. This is so true that even if there were something in the universe that could not be described this way, precisely because of this, it could be described this way, for then the universe would be divided into two symmetrical opposing groups - things that can be described with Yin and Yang and things that cannot be described with Yin and Yang - and there you have Yin and Yang in its entirety.

Pay attention (!) that the same unique specificity of relativity exists here: every opposite is the exact opposite only of one thing, and every pair of Yin and Yang materializes only based on checking their presence. For example, a just action can be the opposite of an unjust action in one relative test plane, but that same action can be foolish (and therefore the opposite of wise) in another relative test plane. We are well acquainted with this from driving on the road; many times, we are just but not entirely wise - and here before us are two specific sets of Yin-Yang related to the same action; the question is only what we sought to find or measure, what we chose to relate to, or in other words - what we chose to pay attention to.

The second important thing about Yin and Yang is their dependence on each other. One does not exist without the other. Yin is the contour of Yang, and vice versa. Yin is everything that is not Yang, and Yang is everything that is not Yin. Why is this important? Because if everything has its opposite and the opposite is exactly what defines the thing itself, then "isness" does not emerge from chaos merely in response to a specific temporary utility but has no choice but to exist simply because it has an opposite; if there is chaos, there must immediately be the opposite of chaos, and that is "isness", for otherwise, even chaos would not exist. These two principles of Yin and Yang are valid and exist at every scale in the universe—from the smallest particle to the entire cosmos.

According to "the Ari" (Rabbi Isaac ben Solomon Luria, the greatest Kabbalist of Safed in the 16th century), God "cleared a space" within Himself to allow for the creation of the world, that is, the creation of reality external to the divine infinity. Pay attention (!) that the finite world that was created is not the opposite of the infinite world. According to the Ari, the divine infinity is not a "thing" at all. It is not the chaotic slackness we are talking about here, that raw formless potentiality of all information. According to the Ari, the divine infinity is beyond any definition, no matter how abstract. It cannot be spoken of at all, and precisely because of this, it was first necessary to create within the infinity a sort of empty space that is indeed the opposite of "what is" - and this empty space is exactly our chaotic slackness, the template of chaos into which existence is poured.

Let's not be tempted into the convoluted rabbit hole of discussing God or the creation of the universe. We will soon find ourselves in an endless maze of frustrations, paradoxes, and recursions, whether we take the scientific approach, the religious-spiritual approach, or any other. The universe, as the greatest "what is," is mentioned here only to present a scale: the processing action we call "attention" occurs in the "what is" at all its levels, from a particle to the entire cosmos. Let's say just one small thing, nevertheless, because we cannot ignore the beautiful aesthetics of the match: try to imagine the Yin-Yang movement of the necessity of the "non-universe" to become the "universe." How does it appear in your imagination? What does it look like? Is it something slow, gradual, and procedural? Or maybe something fast, explosive, expanding rapidly? Some kind of... Bang?

The third important principle embodied in the philosophy of Yin-Yang is that within every Yin, there is a tiny piece of Yang (and vice versa). If we look at the symbol, we see that Yin has a "Yang eye" and Yang has a "Yin eye." Each does not only define its opposite by its contour, but also contains a measure of it within itself. The meaning of this principle is that each side does not represent an absolute, one-sided entity. The identity of everything is also composed of the presence of its exact opposite within it.

So, what is an "entity"? What is a "thing"? How can we measure its significance, its value? There are two ways to do this; one is to measure what the thing is made of, what is in it. We can call this the "Yang value" of the thing. The other way is to measure the thing based on the opposite of everything it is not. We can call this the "Yin value" of the thing. Practically, it is impossible to measure something by its Yin value because the opposite of anything is essentially the entire universe, known and unknown, minus the thing. However, the Yin method is much more accurate than the Yang method for several reasons: First, it is purer. It truly measures all the components of the thing simultaneously. For example, when measuring the Yang value of the entity "Ido," it is very difficult to say something that is not extremely limiting. My Yang values are very scarce; I am a man, I have brown eyes, a bald head, I am 1.74 meters tall, and so on and so forth. But in my Yin values, you can say not only that I am not the opposite of all these, meaning I am "not a woman," "not blue-eyed," or "not hairy in my head."

Here you can say about me that I am also "not a stone," "not the planet Saturn," "not a clothespin," "not Barack Obama" - and continue on and on to almost infinity. So maybe it would be utterly impractical to list my Yin values on my identity card, but on the other hand, it would be much more accurate than just saying what I am. Moreover, in the Yin value method, the "oceanic" truth that language hides is more prominently present, the truth that lies beyond the curtains of consciousness, which is that there is actually no separation between one thing and another and that the difference between me and the rest of the things in the universe stands naked and false, and only the fig leaf of utilitarianism slightly covers it. The Yin value shows us that there is a fundamental connection of identity between every entity because the "Yin eye" of every thing contains a kind of reflection of all the rest of the universe, which is the opposite of the thing, and the presence of the opposite within the thing is an actual part of its definition, of what "it" is.

I remember once my eldest daughter Yaheli and I were sitting on a bench on the street while waiting for the start of some class, and we looked at the passersby when suddenly, and all at once, we were struck by the realization that we were actually looking, through them, at all the people in the world. After all, every person we saw had seen other people that day. This interaction between them, even if it was just a glance, was retained somewhere in their brain, and they carried it now with them, it even changed them in the sense that it was now somehow part of who they were. And every one of the people that person saw had seen other people, and so on and so on - meaning that to a considerable extent, there is an imprinted impression of all people in every person at any given moment. And even if there is a person who no one saw that day (because he is isolated or imprisoned, for example) - still, someone thought about that person somewhere in the world, and that person met other people who met other people - and this chained gaze reached straight to us on the bench. In those days, I still didn't know the Buddhist concept of "dependent origination" ("pattica-samuppada"), but today I know that according to this view, every phenomenon comes into being together with and because of other phenomena, and all phenomena are interconnected like a web. This web is called by Buddhists "The Indra Net." Imagine a kind of infinite web of threads with a dewdrop hanging at each junction, in which all the other drops are reflected. These dewdrops are "things," and we humans are part of them too. We are not independently separate and fixed from other things. We are intertwined with the entire universe and reflect it, and the entire universe reflects us, and thus we actually reflect ourselves in an infinite recursion.

These two philosophical ideas of Yin-Yang and Indra's net express the complexity of the identity of everything that exists. If we apply this to the attention string system, we will find that the very holding of each side at the end of the string is already a kind of recognition of the existence of the other side - and that this recognition is a result of the existence of the other side within it, of its "eye."

In conclusion, if we look deeply into the main movement of attention from the element of chaos (the abstract Yin data) to the element of being (the concrete Yang information), we see that it is an action of bringing into presence. Presence is the result of attention. This happens when the mother mouse pays attention to her son and through her touch brings into presence both him and herself standing beside him, as well as the interaction between them, thereby generating in him a sense of security that protects him from the anxiety surrounding him. In this sense, the trauma experienced by the mouse is actually a template of chaos, the opposite of the mother's touch, into which the touch is poured "with utmost perfection"; this also happens on the particle level when the neuron in the mouse's brain pays attention to his mother's touch and responds to it in a way that generates a chain of actions and reactions in his genetic system. It also happens when apples fall on physicists' heads when space and time, those relative coordinates, pay attention to mass of matter: this is gravity. It happens in evolution when the individual randomly or not responds to an environment – although the purpose of presence is not evolution; it is not survival, continuity, or development. Presence precedes these just as attention precedes discernment. The purpose of presence is to be, or to become, as opposed to not be, or, more accurately, its purpose is to be with concrete meaning, with value - and all the meaning lies in the relationship between the two holders of the string, in their interaction.

If we take another step in this line of thought, we will find that from the perspective of attention, we cannot say that the world exists; it is present. If "things" are indeed created by virtue of their interaction because only that grants them concrete value and meaning - then the subjective is what creates the objective. Reality as we describe it here is not composed of laws and objects that obey them while they interact. No. The interaction precedes the things.

The philosopher Immanuel Kant distinguished between the subjective world of phenomena and the objective things-in-themselves, stating that we cannot have access to the objective as it is because any examination of the objective passes through the subjective. But what is the subjective? Who is the subject that measures, observes, and seeks to know the objective? If there are no things, to whom does the gaze belong? According to our attention-based approach, the objective is actually the phenomenon. The objective is the relative, the "thing" we produce in our consciousness. The paradox in Kant's method is that the thought that there is an objective thing at all is a thought that is clearly not objective. What we truly do not have access to is the subjective - because the subject is not fixed and separate; it is swept along in an endless stream of interactions.

Seemingly, we are unable to grasp the true essence of an abstract concept like "love." We can only grasp the visible, concrete aspect present in the love of a particular person for another person; we use the concrete to explain the abstract to ourselves. But what is the concrete if not a utilitarian decision we made about something that has no boundary, just like the table we presented in the introduction to this essay? Is there anything more objective than what is abstract and undefined? Is the data not more objective than the concrete information derived from it? Is the value not more dubious than the equation? And thus, is presence, which is the result of interaction, not more real than hermetic, sterile existence? Is there even such existence at all? Is the interaction not the only truth?

In contrast to Kant, Leibniz coined the term "monad" as a logical derivative of the insight that there is no material; Leibniz claimed that a monad is a kind of "atom of existence" that is non-material, a schema of a fundamental unit of reality, but argued that a monad "has no windows," meaning it cannot be in relation to anything, precisely because of that assertion about matter and things which do not exist because they are in endless relations or interactions with each other. Attention, on the other hand, presents us only with windows. There is nothing but relations. The relation itself is the most basic unit of existence. Its movement is attention, which is the engine of the mechanism that processes abstract data into concrete information, and the "product" it creates is presence.

A series of Tensions

(The Tension Rises)

Chapter One: Identification

Like the reflections on the Indra net, reality is filled with countless "slack" systems of attention. Slackness is the first chapter in the tension series of the attention string, a series of five chapters that ends in bringing the interaction into presence, that is, to produce a response. Slackness is not detachment; because everything contains within it at least a small hint of everything that is its opposite, every slackness already reflects a given state that can be defined as the basic identification of the attention sender with its recipient.

This basic identification is not a circumstantial event. It is not a link in a chain of reactions. It happens all the time and actually does not happen but exists outside the measurable physical, binary, classical plane, in that pre-concrete plane where superposition exists. To explain this, we will need a special number: zero.

Today, in the Consciousness Research Department at Tel Aviv University, a fascinating study is being conducted related to this peculiar number, a study aimed at creating nothing less than a new mathematics. This mathematics, conceived by Dr. Moshe Klein and Professor Oded Maimon, is based on an intriguing principle: the perception that zero is not a single number but an entire axis of numbers.

If we divide a number by itself, the result is always 1. But what happens when we divide 0 by 0? Classical mathematics considers this operation an error because it does not yield a logical result. But let's try to ask it differently by reversing the equation.

When multiplying any number by 1, the result is always the number itself. 4 times 1 is 4, 8 times 1 is 8, and so on. If we take the same reversal of the equation to 0: if any number multiplied by 0 is 0, then 0 divided by 0 is essentially every number.

Klein and Maimon argue that there is a difference between the multiples of zero by different numbers. According to their mathematics, 3 times 0 is not equal to 4 times 0. The classical result is indeed 0, but according to their mathematics, which they call "soft mathematics," each case represents a different 0. All the different zeros, which are the result of multiplying all numbers by zero, can be placed on an infinite axis (positive and negative) that Klein and Maimon call the "zero axis." The purpose of the zero axis is not to contradict classical mathematics or nullify it. It seeks to add another dimension through which things can be viewed in a richer way. This dimension is what physicist John Stewart Bell called "Nonlocality" when he explained how quantum entanglement occurs, that is, how the measurement of one particle out of a pair of entangled particles immediately affects its pair even if the two particles are a galaxy apart. Nobel Prize winners in Physics for 2022, Alain Aspect, John F. Clauser, and Anton Zeilinger, proved the existence of this dimension and thereby denied what is called "local realism," where one thing affects another only if there is direct contact between them. Klein and Maimon argue that in this dimension, it is possible to unite mathematics with consciousness, thereby answering Chalmers' call to integrate consciousness as a central force in reality, one that cannot be ignored even when dealing with rigorous and precise sciences. How is this done? Let's try to simplify things. The following example is not directly related to the zero axis but demonstrates how a number whose classical value remains constant can have its conscious value change:

John is a novice farmer. He is very interested in raising chickens. He has acquired all the necessary equipment to be a professional farmer—a tractor, coops, fences, and various tools—but has not yet raised a single chicken. Mathematically, John has 0 chickens. On the other hand, Fred is already an experienced farmer. If we enter his coop and count all the chickens he currently owns, we will find 100 healthy and good chickens.

One night, thieves broke into Fred's farm and stole all his chickens. Now Fred is left with 0 chickens, just like John. But is Fred 's 0 equal to John's 0? In classical mathematics, certainly. Neither of them has chickens, so the value of the chickens they each have is equal. But in terms of consciousness, this is a completely different 0. John's 0 is full of hope and eagerness to grow, while Fred's 0 is full of disappointment, frustration, and longing for everything he has lost. What differs between these two zeros is their conscious value, that is, the intention charged in the number.

Chapter Two: Intention

Imagine a baby standing in front of his father and raising his hands. This is sort of what the template of chaos looks like. There is no actual hug yet, but the intention of the hug is very much present. This is how it works with our slack string.

Intention can increase identification but can also decrease it. If, for example, the baby's father has experienced some trauma related to hugging or touch, his identification with his son raising his hands toward him might decrease, and he might withdraw.

Intention is not a reactive action. A reaction, according to the dictionary definition, is "an action that comes in response to a stimulus." Like identification, the intention to stretch charged in the attention string does not exist in the classical physical plane and is not preceded by a stimulus because it is not real itself. The force driving the intention is an imaginary force, much like the concept Einstein devised to differentiate his perception of gravity from Newton's. Unlike a real force (like electricity), an imaginary force does not result from direct interaction between objects but from the relationship between the objects and the observer. The speed of a train relative to a person riding a bicycle next to it is an imaginary force because the speed is not objective but depends on the relationship between the train and the cyclist. When a reductionist describes the reaction of a particle and attributes it to its coding, he describes a real force. When we talk about the force charging the intention in the attention string, we are talking about an imaginary force. In the scenario of the rider and the train, there are a few basic real conditions for the measurement of the imaginary force of the relative speed to be possible at all – there must be a specific rider, there must be a specific train, and they must move alongside each other in a very specific manner. In the transition from the default slackness of the attention string to the slackness charged with intention, the conditions are different altogether because here the interaction precedes the things themselves.

Think about the interaction between two billiard balls hitting each other versus the interaction between two dewdrops on Indra's net reflecting each other. In the string metaphor, the two sides holding it are the dewdrops, the string is the thread, the identification is the reflection, and the intention is the gaze. In a state of slackness, the sides already reflect each other (this is the fundamental identification present in everything), but their eyes are closed. They only reflect but do not look at each other, so the reflection has no validity. When the intention is charged in the string, the gaze is open, and the identification gains validity. But if that gaze itself is not an action, it is also not created. The gaze is simply the Yang of the non-gaze; they are one, and neither precedes the other. In quantum entanglement, the collapse of the superposition of particle x is not a local result of the collapse of the superposition of particle y entangled with it, so it occurs not quicker than the speed of light but outside of it; it happens not in the same second – because a second is a unit of time, and time is local, it is the road on which the cause moves towards the effect – but exactly at that moment, a moment without time, so much so that it can be said that it does not even really "happen" but simply "is" out of necessity, just like that ancient necessity of the "non-universe" to become "the universe" at the moment of the Big Bang, because these two occurrences just "be" outside of time.

The biologist and author Terence McKenna used to joke about the scientific explanations for the creation of the universe: "Give us one miracle," say the scientists according to McKenna, "and we will explain the rest." The gaze is exactly that "miracle." When we ask the question "Why is intention charged in the attention string," we are asking a wrong question because we are talking about time. We are seeking a cause. But the gaze that opens is not a "something" gaze. It is a nothing gaze. Our universe flickers like a film in a projector. When we watch a movie, half the time we are in darkness. Between the frames of something, there is a chasm of nothing. Unlike the collapse of the quantum superposition, where something sends a measurement gaze towards nothing, in charging the intention in the attention string, it is the nothing that seeks to measure. Whom? Itself. Why? This is a somewhat barren question because it, too, seeks to force a needle of causality out of a timeless haystack. But if we try to extract an answer to satisfy the imagination, it would be: to continue being nothing. Because without something that is, there would be no opposite of it, which is what that something is not. Without Yang, there is no Yin. No-thing is an inseparable part of some-thing; it is its causeless necessity. Its cause is itself, the interaction between them – attention.

And we can also think of it this way: Are you familiar with those art pieces made of abstract-shaped pieces of paper stuck on wire rods which are then stuck on some plane? If you look at such a piece, you get a kind of "cotton field" of random shapes. But if you turn on a flashlight and point it at that field at a certain angle – suddenly, a silhouette in a very distinct shape (e.g., Jesus, Elvis, LeBron James, a swan, etc.) appears. Attention is the interaction between abstract data pieces, and intention is the context in which those data pieces are tied together, a context that will eventually lead to a very concrete piece of information, just as the flashlight connects the abstract shapes and turns them into a concrete silhouette on the wall. Intention does not have to be an expression of any will – it is a natural property, inherent in everything. Precisely because of this, when our brain processes the abstract data of photons bouncing off some object, say a flower, it does so because our brain seeks a context for that data. We cannot deal with cognitive dissonances, only consonants – therefore, our brain will always seek context, and hence it is the most sophisticated attention-processing machine nature has to offer. But not only the brain. Intention, or the aspiration for context, is present in everything.

Chapter Three: Stretching

After the slack string is charged with the intention to stretch, the actual stretching begins. During the stretching, the identification increases. Pay attention (!): We are still not in full attention. The string is still not properly taut, and things have not yet been "cut to the utmost perfection" into their chaos template.

When asked how he created his famous sculpture called "The Dog" – a sculpture of a thin, scruffy dog whose body seems composed of a pile of burnt matches – the sculptor Alberto Giacometti replied that he walked down the street, saw the dog, and instantly became him. Such identification is not reflective; it is merely a touch of the representation of the dog in his soul, a one-sided representation: "Giacometti is the dog," but "the dog is not Giacometti" because the dog does not respond to Giacometti's identification in the same way; it does not recognize any aspect of Giacometti in its soul. In contrast, reflective identification is always two-sided. This is Mise en abyme (French for "placing into infinity") – reflection within reflection. The form of projection from one side of the string to the other is "Möbius-like," meaning like in a Möbius strip, the paradoxical loop with two dimensions but only one side. The two dimensions are the two entities holding the string, and the one side is the infinite interaction of a mirror with another mirror standing opposite it. As such identification grows, the string stretches: what was chaos becomes present. Pay attention (!): The recipient's identification with the sender sharpens their separate identities. There is no better proof that everything is defined by its opposite; from identification arises separation. From the lack of language arises language. From chaos arises presence.

The act of stretching is the heart of data processing; here the abstract slowly becomes concrete. The Möbius interaction between the sender and recipient of attention is what generates this transformation by its very nature: the relativity between the sender and recipient creates "contextualization" of values to data. Just as one cannot say a tree is "small" except in relation to a larger tree, so attention shapes the chaos template of the interaction by that Möbius echo. Data meets other data and they echo each other, with each echo exponentially refining the interaction until a "cut to the utmost perfection" template of chaos is created within which the data can be dressed in the unique information that is the unique essence of the interaction.

Pay attention (!) that the data being contextualized is only seemingly local data, meaning the data associated with the unique interaction between the sender and recipient. In fact, each such interaction is a Möbius singularity of the entire universe with itself precisely because there are no "things"; the meeting of the sender and recipient is only a spark in an ongoing trail of interactions that began at the beginning of time itself. In this sense, the movement of the interaction does not occur on an external plane of space and time because space and time are inherent parts of the fabric of reality of the universe that the sender and recipient represent, each from their unique perspective; space and time are not separate from the sender and recipient. This is a distinctly Leibnizian statement, although its application through the prism of attention slightly adorns the things Leibniz said: space and time are properties of the sender and recipient themselves; otherwise, there could be no angle at all, no relativity.

Chapter Four: Tension

When the string is taut to exactly the right degree, we are finally in full attention. We are the mother mouse paying attention to her anxious son – but have not yet touched him; or, from the perspective of the neuron after the touch is given – we are paying attention to the touch – but have not yet fired.

Chapter Five: Response

What is a response? The neuron's response in the mouse's brain is to fire its command. The genes' response in the mouse's body is to reorganize. The mouse's response as a whole conscious body is to relax and feel secure. The father will hug his son. The metal will react to ultraviolet light. Spacetime will respond to the mass of matter. A response comes only after attention; attention precedes response.

But it doesn't end here.

Forgetfulness

I look at the words I wrote, and they distance themselves from me. Goethe wrote: "Alles nahe werde fern" (in German – "Everything near becomes distant"). In contrast, the Israeli playwright, poet, and author Hanoch Levin wrote in one of his poems: "Where have gone you-before-you-came?" Levin describes a man waiting for a woman to arrive with great longing, but when she finally shows up, the longing fades, and now he remains yearning for the image of her before she came – before she was present. Here too, the distance gave birth to closeness, and the closeness gave birth to distance.

In the previous chapter, we saw how from identification is born distinction, and from distinction also separation. We talked about Yin-Yang and how it is necessary for everything to have its opposite. Does this mean that everything that is made present – and precisely because it is made present – is doomed to return to chaos? Take, for example, a baby. The baby exists and could not exist without the intention to bring a baby into being (conscious or not), meaning that the baby "poured" into the template of chaos, which is "the world without the baby," and not just any baby but "the world without this specific baby." But even "the world without this specific baby" is not just a template but also content because it itself poured into a template of chaos, which is "the world without the world without this specific baby" – and on the other side, the baby who "is" is immediately also a template of chaos itself, a slack string that will be stretched in due course into various systems of attention. The relationship of Yin and Yang is continuous and infinite on the Möbius strip plane; like in the drawing of the Dutch artist M.C. Escher "Drawing Hands," where two hands each hold a pencil and draw one another – being shapes non-being, which shapes being. This is a necessity because the "things" produced by interactions do not fixate into separate and unchanging selves; the dust that the table will become will also continue to change through subsequent interactions; it is not "dust" either. Bringing into presence is not a truth. It is just a foggy station on the way from one interaction to the next. From these words, it is almost possible to say that interactions are the essential "beings" of existence, while things – all matter, including us – are merely carriers serving them for their survival. Chaos seeks to become through us. The abstract seeks to be present through the concrete. This is a somewhat gloomy thought for us because it seemingly leaves us subject to another's dominion, and unlike particles or systems with less complex consciousness than ours, we care.

While writing these words, there is still a lively and vigorous debate about the existence of free will. On one side of the divide, dualists believe that free will indeed exists because there is a soul or spirit separate from the physical body, and due to their distance and disconnection from the limitations of matter, they can influence it. In contrast, reductionists advócate causal determinism, meaning the belief that every result has an explainable cause that can be reduced to a physical phenomenon, to matter, and based on the belief that nothing is not matter, they deny the possibility of free will influencing matter from the outside. Neither side has doubt; they only struggle against each other. The doubt echoes only in the rooms of the "middle people," those who seek on the one hand to rely on empirical facts and on the other not to dismiss the place of consciousness in which the experience of free will exists because within that same consciousness exists the empirical reductionist measurement itself, a measurement that ultimately, and necessarily, gropes for the objective from within the subjective. But if the world indeed does not exist but is present, perhaps it is worth changing the essence of the discussion and replacing the term "free will" with the term "bringing into presence."

When we talk about free will, we talk about the feeling that we are the exclusive owners of our decisions, that they are made by us and by us alone - that we choose them. But what is a decision, and what is a choice? Seemingly, a choice is the result of the assumption that more than one possibility truly exists, but in fact, it is the result of an earlier assumption that there is any possibility at all. When we stand at a crossroads in a "real" world, every path to which the crossroads splits is an object with its own properties independent of anything else, including the person taking it. Let us not forget that in such a world, the person taking the path is also an object, as are his thoughts and feelings. This is precisely the flaw in the concept of free will: there is no place for the subject to influence the equation because there is essentially nothing that is not an object. But if the world indeed does not exist but is present, and presence is the relative meeting point of subjects seeking to measure each other, then it would be more accurate to say that there is nothing that is not a subject - the crossroads, the paths, and I, the person taking them - we are all in mutual influence on one another. "Right" and "left" do not exist in and of themselves, and therefore the possibility of choosing between them is an illusion, not due to some materialistic determinism that asserts the choice has already been made for us by a causal chain whose links and connections are entirely inaccessible to us. No, the problem is not in the "freedom" of the will but in the will itself, which does not exist because will is an expression of an object towards an object and not of a subject towards a subject - I, the separate one, seek the other separate one - while in the reality of attention and bringing into presence, the meaning of separation is not independence but rather the reinforcement of the interaction of the relationship. And as we have already noted, this is only a station on the way to the next interaction.

So what can we do after all? In a present world, are we doomed to live a life of (experienced) slavery under the arms of interactions? Are we, like someone caught to a paddleball game on the beach, supposed to just bend down and let the balls of chaos and being pass over our heads? Or is there some special way in which we can still be part of the game?

According to Jewish Halacha, the laws in the Torah, field owners are obligated to leave or give parts of their yield to the poor. These parts are called "gifts for the poor," and the commandment mainly concerns three actions related to the yield: gleanings, forgotten sheaves, and the corners of the field. "Corners" means not to harvest the corners of the field but to leave them for the poor so they can harvest them and collect their yield. "Gleanings" means that if a sheaf falls during the harvest, it is not to be picked up. But what is "forgotten sheaves"? Seemingly, it means that if a sheaf was forgotten in the field, it is not to be returned to. But then the question arises - if the sheaf was indeed forgotten, why would we want to return to it at all? And on the other hand, if we remember that we forgot - we are no longer forgetting. There is no escape - one who seeks to fulfill all three commandments must somehow manage to forget intentionally. But how can one actively engage in forgetting?

Our default state is forgetfulness. We do not remember, for example, all the people who passed by us on the street or everything that has ever been said to us. If we remembered everything, we would go insane. But if something special happened, if someone suddenly shouted or behaved strangely, if some event was specially marked in our minds - we will remember it. For example, I vividly remember the neighbor's mischievous son from my childhood. Why him specifically? Because one day we walked toward each other in the passage leading to the entrance of the house, and just as he passed me, he decided to play a prank and scare me with a horrifying scream. That scream etched the event into my memory. Another thing I remember from childhood is my father, who was an exceptional scholar and even held the title of "champion of champions" on the popular trivia show "Master Mind," teaching me a special method for memorizing long lists of items: all you have to do is associate each item with a funny visualization so that it easily imprints in your mind. In short - we forget everything that does not make an effort for us to remember it.

Therefore, when we make an effort not to forget a single sheaf in the field, we are doing something very unnatural. To remember, we mark the harvesting event with the artificial thought that if we do not make an effort to gather everything, we might be left with nothing. If we look deeply into this thought, its essence is that we perceive ourselves as the sole responsible for what we have or do not have. We are in control of the abundance in our lives - and this is exactly what we are commanded to forget because the truth is that this control is nothing but a gross lie, an illusion. We cannot even know what will happen in the next moment. We are helpless. We depend on the mercy of forces greater than ourselves, just like the poor for whom this commandment ostensibly exists. It is not by chance that the verse ends with the words "and you shall remember that you were a slave in the land of Egypt"; the intention is not that we remember that we were once poor and therefore now that we are well-off we should give to those less fortunate than us. No - we are still poor now, and the control we try to achieve over our lives is as artificial as the false power it grants us. If we can internalize this, we can truly forget those sheaves in the field because they will no longer be marked by our anxiety over their loss.

So we can forget, meaning - we can stop trying to remember. Without external intervention, everything tends to disintegrate, scatter, return to entropic disorder - return to chaos. Without actively working to maintain it, the presence that attention created will fade. But it does not fade back into the chaos from which it came; this is an evolution of the interaction to the next one.

In Douglas Adams' wonderful book "The Hitchhiker's Guide to the Galaxy," one of the characters instructs the main protagonist, Arthur, on how to fly:

> *"In order to fly, one must simply miss the ground."*

The ground that Arthur must miss is the mind. To forget, we must jump and then let go of the mind; only then can we return to the chaos of the heart and fly. Letting go of the mind is letting go of possibilities. This means giving up language to return to what lies beyond language, to the place Bialik wrote about, where the whole purpose of language is to cover and conceal. As the Chinese philosopher Zhuangzi, who lived in the 4th century BCE, wrote:

> *The fish trap exists because of the fish; once you've gotten the fish, you can forget the trap. The rabbit snare exists because of the rabbit; once you've gotten the rabbit, you can forget the snare. Words exist because of meaning; once you've gotten the meaning, you can forget the words. Where can I find a man who has forgotten words so I can have a word with him?*

We are doing this right now. We are trying to achieve the letting go of the mind through the mind. But let's not forget that this is a "Möbius process": to achieve the letting go of the mind through the mind, we must first let go of the mind. To use the trap, we must first equip ourselves with it, but to equip ourselves with it, we must first be without a trap, not just any trap, but precisely this trap. This is the template of chaos into which things are "cut to the utmost perfection."

Unlike a choice stemming from free will, in the choice to "let go of the trap" to bring reality into presence (and ourselves within it as part of it), there is almost no will, or at least the will has no expression because the only will inherent in it is devoid of the desire to influence or change; it merely seeks to be. There is no active action of doing here, but rather of giving up, almost surrendering: we let go of the tool through which the interaction was created, that is, language, senses, definitions, and allow ourselves to dwell in the pure meaning itself.

Part Two

Inward

Pay Attention

My beloved son. I don't know what is right and what is wrong. For example, whether it is more correct to write "I do not know" or "what is not correct." In the material world, there is only one crevice intended for this book, and every letter might invalidate the form from the space. What I do know is: things are not things. I look to the horizon, and my mother's image is a shadow. But the horizon is a flower, and my mother is water, and I am the moon, and the gaze is a mirror. This unstory is what I wish to give you, my son. Like a photograph of a locked box with a musical instrument inside. Not the story of the musician. Not the story of the instrument. Not the music and not even the lock. Just the box. Almost not even the box, but its form. This thing is very dear to me. But I do not know how it can be said.

This paragraph is taken from the book "Ma" (2022, Tangier Publishing), which I wrote and dedicated to my son Zohar and to my late mother. The word "Ma" in Japanese symbolizes the space between things, a space that is not empty but has a meaning no less significant than the things it separates, like the silence between notes in a musical piece, like the Yin eye in the Yang body, or like the space between written words. This un-story is everything that is not found in the concrete story of reality but defines it no less, and perhaps even more, than words and language.

The second part of this essay's heartbeat deals with such a "Ma," in that strange place where, in order to enrich the relationship between the sender of attention and its recipient, the "being" that was brought into presence is stripped away, and the meaning makes a U-turn into the chaos, into the heart. This is a natural process, and it occurs effortlessly in systems with low or infinitesimal consciousness. We, with our complex consciousness, need to "pay attention" to it, focus our spotlight of discernment on it to allow it to happen for us not only objectively but also in our experience of the reality around us.

I chose to focus on examples from several fields close to my heart – parenting, therapy, faith, art, and meditation – although what is written can also be applied to many other fields. I hope that each reader can find themselves there as well.

So how do we strip the present from the "being" and return it to chaos, precisely to give greater validity to its presence, to the attention directed at it? The answer, I think, is not singular. The heart is not a place of order or justice. It is not really a place at all – it is what creates a place. What is important for us is to let go of the belief that the more we define ourselves, the more unique and independent we are – the more present and free we will be. If reality is not a reality of "things" but of interactions and connections, then precisely as we let go of "language," the boundary of the separating consciousness, as we pay attention to the connections that continuously and infinitely create who we are not as beings with independent essence but as what we really are – dew drops spread on the infinite net of reality – we will realize that what defines us is not what makes us unique but precisely what is reflected in us, that is, our context and relationship with all the other dew drops. And the more we let go of consciousness back into the Yin abyss, the more we return the attention to the heart – the more present and free we will be also in our experience, in our subjectivity, and the more shall will expand the canvas of our gaze because what was brought into presence was never truly the sender or the recipient; it was the connection between them.

And even if we negate everything written on these pages, even if we say there is no "heart," no chaos, even if all the actions of attention are an illusion originating from neurons firing in our brains and their obedience to the laws of nature is obedience that has nothing to do with data processing – it is still the only tool the external reality (i.e., everything that is not us) has in order to bring itself into presence for us and for us to bring ourselves into presence within it. In this sense, Kant was right: we have no access to this reality without it. In this sense, the choice to be attentive does not stem from some detached "spiritual" free will but from the material itself: we choose not from several possible futures spread before us but from one present. The turn at the junction is not a choice between two paths because we are not walking on the path: we are the path. We do not choose above or separately from reality but as part of it. We pay attention, meaning we experience the attention, and thus use the only interpretation engine we have to process reality – our presence within it and in relation to it. In fact, when we do not pay attention, then we are above and separate from the material because then we "deny validity" to parts of reality and to ourselves standing opposite and within it. This is a kind of "dark spirituality" if you like, in which we do the opposite of bringing into presence, and instead of bringing into being from chaos, we cast into non-being from being, and this time it is absolute non-being, not the chaos that is everything and nothing but the non-being of Parmenides, the non-being that is not. Hence, this is an action of disconnection and reduction. Descartes said: "I think, therefore I am." Well, the meaning of this second part before you is – I pay attention, therefore I am present.

Listening

It has already been written here more than once that universal-creative attention is not related to the same spotlight of discernment we call "focus." Focus is a conscious process related to experience, while attention is a process that is not necessarily related to consciousness and can occur even in "cold" compliance with the laws of nature, as in particles, plants, and so on. A stone does not need the whole process of letting go and forgetting that we are talking about here because a stone does not experience itself as a separate subject from reality in the first place – not that it experiences itself differently, it just lacks experience as far as we can tell. Stones do not need some Bialik-stone to tell them about the barrier of language or a Buddha-stone to tell them about the suffering that consciousness produces because stones do not perceive themselves at all as "stones," and in fact, they are not really "stones" – it is only us who have named them as such.

We, on the other hand, need this letting go because without it, we suffer. If all things are separate from each other, I can control them to change them, and I will do so with all my might to avoid meeting pain; if there are "things," I can control things. However, if things are intertwined, if there are no "things" at all, I cannot change anything, and therefore any attempt to do so will only cause me suffering.

Fortunately, consciousness is the tool that can help us free ourselves from itself. To do this, we need to reduce all background noise and stay as much as possible with... well, nothing.

If you ask Yuval Ido Tal, a wonderful Buddhist teacher and experienced Zen meditation instructor, what the purpose of meditation is, he will simply say: meditation. This is an outrageous answer and, of course, there is no more correct one. We are used to doing things to achieve something else through them; we feel that if we have meditated just for the sake of meditation, if we have gained nothing from it, we have remained the same as we were before, and if so, why should we waste our time on it at all? However, a more meticulous and profound look will show us that it is precisely when we meditate to achieve something else that we change less – and not for the better. If we sought to relax, it is possible that the meditation will help us momentarily, but reality is reality, and after a while, for one reason or another, we will become a little less relaxed and will desperately long to return to meditate to relax, so much so that life without meditation will become a life full of suffering, and soon we will need meditation to free ourselves from the attachment to meditation. But if we just meditated, we gained a few moments where the background noise decreased, and we could be present in the connections with everything that is right at this exact moment. By letting go of the desire to gain, we let go of our separateness because we give up our control over "things" and instead grant validity to our presence as part of our interactions with things. We return things to the heart, and they return not separate from us, but equal – to us, to everything.

Poetry

Heart / Roni Somek

To Shirley, a brain researcher

I am a carpenter
sawing from the flesh of the tree
doors to the chambers of the heart.
On their threshold
lie letters sent by the brain
and within them the secret of the eternal forests
that I so wanted to know.

Roni Somek is an Israeli poet, author, and artist. His poetry has been translated into dozens of languages and has won many awards, locally and internationally; he received the Polish "Order of the Knights of the Cross" and the "Man of the Year" award from the Lions organization, and he holds the title of Knight in the Order of Arts and Letters of the French government. When I published my first novel in 2010, the publishing house invited Roni to the launch event to give a few words. Roni arrived and gave the book (and me) very generous attention. After I got married (for the second time), it turned out that Roni was also my wife's teacher at the seminar where she studied for her special education degree; thus, Roni became a special friend of the family.

Roni speaks poetry. Even when we sat down for a cup of coffee to discuss the manuscript of this essay, there was not a sentence he said to me without a metaphor, synecdoche, or some form of metonymy. If Bialik talks about the covering language uses to hide the frightening uncertainty of chaos, with Roni, everything is almost exposed. The movement between the heart and the brain and back is so natural to him that it is no longer a movement but a place. Therefore, it is easy to use his words to illustrate exactly the heartbeat we are discussing: outward and inward.

Roni writes: "I am a carpenter sawing from the flesh of the tree doors to the chambers of the heart." We can analyze this sentence with our minds and thus deepen our understanding of it. We can note the choice of words and identify with the separation existing in the poem between what is material, the tree from which the pages are made on which the words are written, and the heart and its chambers, which are not made of material but to which we need to install a material door to access them – just like the "empty space" of the Ari, the space that God Himself cleared to allow the finite world to be created, or like the Yin and Yang pointing out that there is nothing without its opposite, or like the many detailed instructions in the Bible regarding the construction of the Temple, precise and meticulously technical instructions about the dimensions of the material – the information – from which the most spiritual place will be built. The path to the abstract passes through the material, the path back to chaos passes through being, and the true validation of the presence that attention has produced for us lies in its release and in listening to the sound produced by the string, that is, not in the things but in the interaction. This is poetry: to part from words with the help of words.

Indeed, Roni's words will not be fully present if we stop at our intellectual insights about them and do not continue beyond. Otherwise, we will be forced, in the name of logic and common sense, to ask how the written words are even possible. What is the meaning of placing "letters from the brain" on the threshold of the door leading to the heart, letters carrying an unspoken secret that is not read but remains in the realm of "I so wanted to know"? To truly understand this, meaning to return the insight to the heart, just like in meditation where we let go of all expectation, we need to stop understanding it. Poetry is un-language. A word like "door" that exists in everyday life to create a utilitarian separation of "door" from everything that is not a door, disintegrates within the poem from its boundaries and limitations. Like the rabbit that has been caught and now the trap that caught it can be forgotten – there is no door, only the meaning of the door. And with this meaning freed from the boundary, the boundaries between all things collapse; between the brain and the heart, between the paper and the words, and perhaps especially between Roni and his daughter.

Love

I am a husband, father, and grandfather. Most of the remaining time, I study Rambam, Aristotle, and Avicenna. Not only because I am good at it, but because I have no choice. Without it, chaos will leave nothing of me.

This year I turned sixty. I lived with the plan that I will teach a certain Rambam book and then teach it a second time because once is barely an introduction, and then we will study Aristotle's physics and metaphysics, and then the hints and remarks of Avicenna. And then there are more things.

This is what Nir Stern, a psychologist, wrote to me when I asked him to tell me how he sees attention in the therapy he provides and asked how he would present himself here. How beautiful it is that through the little that a person writes, one can peek into the person himself. Not only because of what he wrote – but mainly because of what he did not write, because of the Japanese "Ma", that space between the words. And whoever peeks attentively sees not only Nir – but also himself, the reader: This is a wonderful example of the presence of the interaction itself and not of the "things" taking part in it.

For example, Nir did not mention anything about his profession as a therapist here, but the text he wrote demonstrates exactly that – the act of healing and uniting, because when Nir writes simply "And then there are more things," precisely because these things are undefined, something very similar to healing occurs. If he had written, for example, "And then I treat people" or "Once I was ultra-Orthodox" or "I received my certification as a therapist from Rabbi Wolbe" or "I published a book on psychology and Judaism" – where would I, the reader, be in all of this? I wouldn't. There would be Nir, there would be me, and I could look at him from a distance, understand his words – but there would be no "us." I wouldn't be with him, and he wouldn't be with me. "And then there are more things" – I have no choice but to wonder what things. There is a chasm here that no one can fill but me, and if I filled it, I am already a part of it. Part of what was passed to me, part of Nir. I myself am those "more things" of Nir. Like in poetry, when we encounter an image or a sequence of words without linear-logical sense, here too, the gap is the most important component because the one who fills it is the reader, not the writer, and thereby this interaction called "reading" receives special validity, unparalleled and truly present.

Nir explicitly demonstrates this in his unique therapeutic approach. I present his full words here, one by one, because they are precise and valuable not only for this essay and the idea it presents but also for me – as a therapist, as a patient, as a person. Here they are:

> *Maimonides wrote in his books that the masses perceive reality only in material, while the sages perceive reality in the abstract.*
>
> *The precise definition of 'material' – Aristotle wrote in Metaphysics VII, Chapter 7 – is 'definition' (Aristotle's term is 'potential,' but in several places, he explains that it is one and the same. The potential to be different stems from having a definition). What has no definition – means, like when saying the number three is not hot, it does not mean it is cold but that it is entirely outside the definition of hot-cold. Eternity is not a very long time, but it is entirely outside the definition of time.*
>
> *Love is not a defined thing. It is an abstract thing. If a woman asks, "Why do you love me," if the man answers "because you are beautiful," she will ask, "And if I age or get burned and become ugly, will you no longer love me?" And so with wisdom, goodness, and any other attribute and definition. All these are love dependent on something, and it is not true love but*

rather a convenience for me to live with such a woman; it is self-love. Love that is not dependent on anything is a wonder. Why would I love her? And more puzzling – who do I love? If not any of her attributes, then what do I love?

I love the woman not because she is beautiful and wise but because her beauty and wisdom are the expression of my love for her. They are a vessel for the presence of my love in the material world, the world of the masses that demand presence to grasp reality. And thus, I take part in the abstract love that truly exists before I, the defined, love the defined woman.

Attention is the bringing into presence of the abstract in the material world. Attention is the ability of Jacob to perceive Rachel, the abstract Rachel as the non-abstract Rachel. In the abstract, there is no beauty or wisdom, only Rachel as an abstract being. As abstract life. Rachel is a defined person, but she has an element of the abstract. When Jacob pays attention to her, he pays attention not to the abstract – there is nothing in the abstract to pay attention to – but through his attention, he transmits the abstract without nullifying its abstract nature to the defined reality and thus brings it into presence, giving it new existence as defined.

Attention is an act of love. The lover pays attention to his beloved and through his desire for her brings her into presence in a world that can be perceived and related to (this is a fundamental principle that encom-

passes all of nature in all its layers; there is no layer of reality without this).

If a person breaks his hand, the doctor does not heal the bones; he only puts on a cast. Even the person with the broken hand does not heal the bones. What heals is the life force emanating from the abstract. For the life force to apply to the material, the material must be a vessel for it, and this is what the cast does.

The soul can experience splits in countless ways; the split is a common denominator for what seeks healing. The act of therapy only prepares the vessel; the healing comes from the abstract. From love.

The therapist's attention renews a defined reality in the patient – from there, healing arises and spreads and mends. The mending is unification. What was split becomes one. In this unity, the distinction between the giver of attention and the receiver, between the active and the passive, is nullified. In this unity, both the patient and the therapist are created as a complete unity, meaning that from the presence of the mending, from its definition, their separate definitions are nullified. The defined returns to the abstract.

Before sleep, we pray, "Into Your hand I entrust my spirit; You have redeemed me, Lord, God of truth." Redeemed – meaning You have given me attention as one with all others. Thus, the attention I gave returns to me inwardly. The inward is the root of my being in the abstract, in the 'nothingness.' That 'nothingness' from which everything was created as something from nothing. The act of healing lies in this, and it is the healing of both the healer and the healed as one.

But the truth is that even before the mending, another return of the defined to the abstract occurs. In fact, it must occur for the therapy to bear fruit. A therapist must forget what he learned, not even remain with the impression of what was forgotten, but forget everything completely. It is not only impossible and forbidden to try to fit the person in front of me into any model or approach, but I cannot come as someone who knows something, as someone with tools, and expect that our union will lead to any mending.

There is no therapy I perform that does not first heal me before trying to heal the one who comes to me. I receive free therapy every day. The person sits in front of me. I strip myself naked and humiliated as much as possible. He pays attention to my nakedness, and without realizing it, he also strips, and now two naked men sit opposite each other (I do not treat women). Two wrinkled sacks of scrotum that by paying attention to each other become one doubly wrinkled sack.

It is more than relieving loneliness. You can pay attention to a person and be more of him than he is of himself. And he becomes me, a me I did not know, another new me, more me than me. Attention, like a mirror facing a mirror, creates us anew into an undivided human mass. And we see each other in a new light.

> *Sometimes we cry. But the healing, the mending, is in silence. One can be silent quietly, and one can be silent while crying or laughing. Or while we paint each other with the brush of the heart. We sketch with a fine brush the holes in the heart, the violence, the rape, the home. And we cry and laugh. And the silence within all of this melts us, and we feel better. Therapy that does not cause intense joy has no value. The joy, the happiness, is the expansion of attention from person to person when it creates anew like an act of love.*
>
> *I leave the therapy session staggering, bumping into furniture, not knowing where I am or who I am. And so does he. As if we emerge from excessive drinking with a song of drunkards on our lips. And we return to ourselves different from what we were. A bit prophets, a bit mad, and foolish because we forgot. Each one forgot himself and was born to become us.*

This rare ability that Nir speaks of, to strip off the titles of therapist and patient, the healthy and the wounded, the giver and the receiver – is precisely the creation of that "blank page asking to be filled" that we spoke about in the first part of the essay. This is "the string charged with the intention to stretch" in the interaction between those holding its two ends. This is the "empty space." The therapist must allow this gap to fill and realize itself in the unique "we" of him and the patient facing him, and by doing so, mend the fracture and separation that the world of being has produced. Nir speaks of releasing the therapeutic presence, releasing the identities of the therapist and the patient to bring healing to both sides. This is a re-bringing into presence, and it is unique because it is the bringing into presence of unity, the bringing into presence of chaos within the thicket of being, and this round and complete attention is the greatest healing of all.

Ma-thering

Donald Winnicott argued that the formation of a "mental being" in infants is conditioned by the experience of unity or integration that the infant experiences in relation to their primary caregiver (in most cases, the mother). Winnicott saw the infant and the mother as one unit, mother-infant, and asserted that the primary mental processes do not occur in the infant as an independent and separate entity but in this dual-mental unit, the mother and the infant together. For the infant's sense of self to develop authentically (Winnicott divided the self into "false self" and "true self"), the infant must awaken from this illusion of unity and omnipotence only in due time, meaning not too early and not too late. The mother's role is to keep the illusion alive, meaning to nurture the non-separateness from her infant as much as possible: not to demand responses from the infant when he does not want to respond and not to force him to abandon his wishes. According to Winnicott, only an infant who has experienced such a unifying connection can eventually be alone in a healthy way. Winnicott claimed that being alone is not the opposite of connection, but they complement each other. However, there can be unhealthy solitude, just as there can be unhealthy connection, and both are the result of anxiety that develops when the infant does not sufficiently experience this unifying connection. Therefore, the "true self," according to Winnicott, is found, surprisingly, in the connection between subjects. The "true" infant is not the infant himself but is found in the texture of his relations with his mother. Just like in art, where the creation is not found within itself (i.e., in the book, movie, painting, etc.) and not in the mind of the viewer but in the relationship between them, so too, the true self vibrates on the strings of the Indra net more than on any of the dewdrops – or in other words: it exists in the vibration of the string of attention. This is Winnicott in brief.

In the capitalist world we live in, it is hard to imagine a caregiver who nullifies themselves to the extent that they become one with the infant they care for. The "bonding time" we can give our children is very limited – primarily because we must give time to ourselves. Why "must"? Because we are defined by this time precisely, where we develop our careers, our hobbies, our soul. We seek to realize ourselves, meaning the individual, the indivisible, the separate. We are defined by our differentiation from the other, not by our connection to them. And so it is with our children.

Remember the safety instruction videos of airlines before the flight? "In case of a drop in cabin pressure..." These videos always emphasize that the parent should put on the oxygen mask before their child. The child is less capable compared to the adult, so for there to even be an option to save the child, the responsible adult must first save themselves. Sometimes it seems to me that this is the approach also when it comes to the psychological oxygen we give our offspring: a good parent is a healthy parent, a parent who takes care of themselves first and foremost, a parent who is himself before he is a parent, who has his own career, who is fulfilled on all fronts, who holds meaning separate from his role as a caregiver to his children. We tend to think that only such a person can function as a "healthy" parent because otherwise, they would be frustrated, tired, irritable – and who would pay the price for that? The infant, of course. But perhaps the problem lies precisely in the fact that this separateness, the presence that is the result of the attention between these two complex and wonderful systems of parent and child, has not received its full validity because it has not returned to the place from which it came, to the chaos where the parent and child were one?

Like we mentioned earlier, the Ari called his theory of the empty space "the theory of contraction" because the creation of the world was made possible only when God "contracted Himself," literally removed Himself from the place that became "empty" of Him, for otherwise, how could a finite thing be created out of the infinite? Well, maybe it works the other way around too: to return to unity between two independent entities, the independence must "contract" itself, withdraw. Here again – the return to the chaos, to the heart, can only happen with the letting go of attention. And again, we remind ourselves that this is not an emptying, it is not a return to the slack state where there is hardly any identification between the holders of the string. This is a return enriched with the presence of each side, just like that artist who returns at the peak of their development to paint intuitively, but now the intuition is enriched with all the knowledge they have accumulated.

But how can a parent nullify themselves in such a way? Isn't it an impossible concession, even audacious to ask for? Is there even such a thing as "contraction of the self"? Is it really necessary, or maybe the "parent first" approach of the flight oxygen mask is the correct and healthy one?

I am a father myself. I know firsthand the immediate answer to all these questions. No, a parent cannot nullify themselves. Certainly not in the individualistic society we live in. Perhaps not even "contract." Maybe not even just in our society. But there is something in this thought that does not let go of me.

I studied therapy according to the 12-step method. This method has a similar approach to Buddhism in that according to both, the source of human suffering lies in the thirst for control. The person thirsting for control is not thirsting for excessive control or unlimited power, what we call a "control freak." It is a completely normative existence where we all seek to avoid pain or any unpleasant feeling by dimming it, running away from it, or fighting it. Seemingly, this is the most natural and correct thing to do. I got injured? I'll treat the wound. I have a headache? I'll take a pill. But the suffering, which is immeasurably more unpleasant than the pain, lies not in the control but in the thirst. For example: I am stuck in a traffic jam in the middle of the highway. The cars are not moving, and there is no solution in sight. My control over the situation is very limited to nonexistent. And what do I do? I suffer. The thoughts race, the frustration grows – not just because I am in a traffic jam but because this thing prevents me from doing other things, and I feel that if I don't do them, something terrible will happen – someone will be angry at me, I will miss something and as a result, lose an opportunity that could benefit me, other people who need me will fall into distress, and so on. But if for a moment I allow myself to acknowledge the helplessness I am in – not in the sense that I am a victim of the reality I found myself in, but in the deeper sense where I recognize my lack of control over things – maybe only then I will be able to reduce the frustration and anger because they too are an escape from the pain that this helplessness holds. Because if we admit the truth, then even in the place I am in such a hurry to get to, I have much less control than I imagine. Someone will be angry at me at some point. The people who need me will also hurt at some point. I will miss great opportunities at some point. I cannot organize reality exactly as I want almost ever because this reality is made up of countless interactions that are not directly dependent on me. I am helpless. Just as Nir describes the release of the therapist in every therapeutic encounter, so do I release the "therapist of reality" within me in every encounter with reality. I do not stand before it in weakness. I just acknowledge the facts. I change what I can change and release the results of my actions, and thereby my dependence on them. This is "non-being" in the best sense because it does not depend on anything; on the contrary, it allows itself to be part of everything else, to bring into presence all my interactions without trying to influence anything just to avoid some pain. I am part of the traffic jam. I am part of my relationships that embody within them both disappointment, sadness, and frustration, as well as happiness, fulfilment, love. So instead of fighting to change reality, all I need to change is to accept where I am. I need to rest in the "Ma" between the things that are the pieces of the current reality surrounding me.

Maybe it's the same with parenting. When the baby is born, the string of attention between the baby and the parents is stretched to its fullest and resonates with the sound of their separate presence from him (ironically, this happens precisely at the moment of cutting the umbilical cord). In perfect harmony (or perhaps cacophony), the sounds of the parents' separate lives from a moment ago are also heard compared to the lives now standing before them, stained with blood and placenta fragments and screaming helplessly – take me in your arms! – a scream that will be heard frequently in the coming years. Yes, we will stand in this "traffic jam" of parenting for a while. We are helpless against it. But this is also an opportunity. Maybe here too we can delve in the helplessness "actively." Not to be a victim of reality and then try to fight it (in most cases, in vain) – but to release our fear of it and not run away from the pain it will naturally and undoubtedly bring. We will be "good enough parents" by at least not forcing anything, as Winnicott wrote. We will not demand an unnatural response from our children and will not force them to abandon their wishes. We will be in the traffic jam for a moment, or better, in the "Ma" of it, and see that what's jamming things is our thoughts, our thirst for control. Maybe elsewhere someone will be angry with us for not arriving. Maybe we will miss something we considered important and essential. But maybe from this helplessness, from this "ma-thering", a new parenthood will emerge, not based on the separate presence of the baby and the parent and on the boundaries that one draws around the other, but on the release of this separation and the return to the primordial chaos and to a renewed attention that will specifically highlight and bring into presence the connection between them.

I write this and pray for myself as well.

Afterword

Throughout his last years, Albert Einstein unsuccessfully attempted to find a single theory that would unify all other theories – especially his general theory of relativity with quantum mechanics. This journey continues to this day, led by names mentioned here like Rovelli, who proposes concepts such as "relational quantum mechanics" or "loop quantum gravity" to reconcile the existing contradictions between the two old theories of the previous century. Other researchers like Chalmers and Tononi suggest incorporating consciousness as a fundamental component of the laws of nature, thereby adding a new necessary variable to the equations that may illuminate them differently and perhaps lead to the resolution of the persistent conflict.

The idea of panpsychism is also gaining supporters in the scientific community, and as we learned earlier in this essay, the principle of non-locality has already been proven. It seems that science stands on the brink of a singularity of paradigm shift regarding matter and existence.

The idea that attention is present everywhere in the universe, from the smallest particle through evolution in plants and animals, in humans, and even in gravity itself, is not meant to push science beyond this singularity point or disturb the relative-quantum conflict. It certainly cannot resolve it, and it does not even aim to say anything concrete about it. If there is one thing it suggests, it is that this is not a conflict at all. At least not on the plane of attention and the meaning of its actions and purposes.

All the proposed solutions deal with discovery. They seek to discover something that will connect all the disconnected pieces of knowledge. The desired solution seemingly lies in narrowing the gap between the hidden universe and the revealed universe, based on the assumption that the universe operates according to fixed laws, and all we need to do for everything to fall into place and be not only known but also understood, is to discover more of them and more about them. The new discoveries could be quantum gravity, string theory, or anything else. But maybe, just as Bialik said, any discovery is actually the greatest concealment. The language, the word, the knowledge, reveals something about the objects but at the same time covers their essence. Maybe the concealment is more necessary for us than we imagine in the context of our presence in reality. Perhaps they are not just chasms on the knowledge highway over which we must build bridges so that our path to the truth is better paved. Perhaps their important role is precisely in remaining chasms.

I remember watching an interview with director Terry Gilliam ("Brazil," "12 Monkeys," "The Fisher King," "Fear and Loathing in Las Vegas," and more), where he talked about how he perceives the difference between two other directors: Steven Spielberg and Stanley Kubrick. As usual (Gilliam is one of the founders of the hysterical "Monty Python" group), he started with a very "essential" difference: Spielberg has a nicer and bigger house than Kubrick. It's funny, but perhaps not really – after all, Spielberg's films are some of the biggest box-office hits ever, while Kubrick's films, despite all the artistic acclaim they receive from critics, teachers, and film students, did not come close to making similar profits. But then Gilliam noted (more seriously) another difference: Spielberg's films give the viewer answers, while Kubrick's films give them questions. Even Spielberg's more "serious" films that deal with less entertaining subjects, like "The Color Purple," which deals with abuse, or "Schindler's List," which deals with the Holocaust, end with a great sense of optimism and victory: the film is wrapped up for the viewer in a small, shiny package of hope. Kubrick's "2001: A Space Odyssey," on the other hand, leaves viewers not knowing exactly what they just saw. But this lack of knowing, Gilliam suggests, reveals much more than the knowledge itself: the unresolved question embodies a deeper truth than any answer.

What is courage? Is it overcoming fear? Or is it perhaps being present in fear to its fullest? Overcoming fear is an answer. Fearing is a question. Attention is the bringing into presence that occurs by moving from the undefined to the defined – but it does not remain there. As we have seen, it also makes the return journey back to the undefined. The return to the undefined is the true closing of the circle of attention, from which the presence of the thing being attended to is validated – not by its definition but by its unraveling. Attention is not the answer to the question "What is the thing?" Attention is a question itself: What is the thing in me? What am I and the thing? What are we? And perhaps even more than that.

> *Outside the barrier of language, behind its veil, the human spirit, stripped of its verbal shell, is always wondering and wandering. There is no speech and there are no words, only eternal wonder; an eternal "what" frozen on the lips. In truth, there is no place even for that "what" which implies some hope for an answer.*

Yes, even a "what" is too much. The wondering of attention is so pure that it contains no question at all. This is not "uncertainty" as in the uncertainty principle of quantum mechanics. There is no unanswered answer here. It is simple being devoid of knowledge. The full movement of attention is presence, and presence is being – but not just being, for attention gives birth to connection: the barrier of language falls, a gaze mirrors a reflected gaze. Attention is being one.

www.ingramcontent.com/pod-product-compliance
Lightning Source LLC
LaVergne TN
LVHW091027150826
845672LV00006BA/1716

* 9 7 9 8 8 9 3 8 3 7 7 0 4 *